**THE ONLY AUTHORITATIVE, COMPREHENSIVE
GUIDE FOR CAT OWNERS
THAT ANSWERS THE QUESTIONS YOU WERE
AFRAID TO ASK . . . WITH THE TRUTH!**

The figures are in. America's favorite pet is the cat. Now the millions of people who know that Puff is every bit as smart as the neighbor's four-year-old—and a whole lot cuter—have the handbook they've been waiting for.

It's the purr-fect way to discover—

- The difference between a cat owner and a bond slave (there is none)

- Top-secret tips on giving away a litter of kittens

- The basic types of cats (The Tramp; The Couch Potato; The Galloping Gourmand)

- The Basic types of cat owners (The Cat-a-holic; The Black Cat Owner; The Soft Touch)

. . . and many, many more fur-ociously funny facts about Cats— and the Owners Who Love Them.

The Unofficial Cat Owner's Handbook

The Unofficial Cat Owner's Handbook

by
Art and Norma Peterson

Illustrations by Cindy Chan

A PLUME BOOK

PLUME
Published by the Penguin Group
Penguin Books USA Inc., 375 Hudson Street,
New York, New York 10014, U.S.A.
Penguin Books Ltd, 27 Wrights Lane,
London W8 5TZ, England
Penguin Books Australia Ltd, Ringwood,
Victoria, Australia
Penguin Books Canada Ltd, 2801 John Street,
Markham, Ontario, Canada L3R 1B4
Penguin Books (N.Z.) Ltd, 182–190 Wairau Road,
Auckland 10, New Zealand

Penguin Books Ltd Registered Offices:
Harmondsworth, Middlesex, England

First published by Plume, an imprint of New American Library, a division of
Penguin Books USA Inc.

First Printing, November, 1990
10 9 8 7 6 5 4 3 2 1

 REGISTERED TRADEMARK—MARCA REGISTRADA

LIBRARY OF CONGRESS CATALOGING-IN-PUBLICATION DATA:
Peterson, Art.
    The unofficial cat owner's handbook / by Art and Norma Peterson ;
illustrations by Cindy Chan.
        p.   cm.
    ISBN 0-452-26518-5
    1. Cats. 2   I. Peterson, Norma, II. Title.
SF447.P467   1990
636.8—dc20   90-35362
                                                          CIP

Printed in the United States of America
Set in Times Roman
Designed by Leonard Telesca

BOOKS ARE AVAILABLE AT QUANTITY DISCOUNTS WHEN USED TO PROMOTE PRODUCTS
OR SERVICES. FOR INFORMATION PLEASE WRITE TO PREMIUM MARKETING DIVISION,
PENGUIN BOOKS USA INC., 375 HUDSON STREET, NEW YORK, NEW YORK 10014.

To Max and Magnolia

Contents

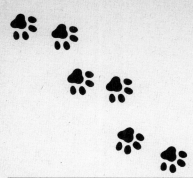

Cat·Own·er 1. Human being who takes responsibility for the care, feeding, and cosseting of a small, furry mammal whose idea of a good time includes twenty-three-hour naps and hot-and-cold running tuna. *See* bond slave. 2. Human being who, coming upon Sylvester coughing up the world's largest fur ball on the Oriental carpet in a room full of cocktail party guests, feels sorry for Sylvester. *See* patsy. 3. Human being who is resigned to waiting another twenty years before replacing the couch, because by then Muffy will have "worked through" her little chintz-shredding fetish. *Similar to* mother. *See also* martyr.

CHAPTER 1

Before You Pick Up That Adorable Ball of Fur . . .

Nine Reasons to Own a Cat

You're in front of McDonald's. A nine-year-old kid is sitting next to a cardboard box with a hand-lettered sign: "Free Kittens." You stop and smile at the cute little balls of fluff, but that's it. You walk on. This child is offering you a small creature to fill your hours with pleasure and amuse-ment and you go scampering off as if the kid is selling acid rain cocktails.

But wait. Slow down. There are several semirational reasons to own a cat. If any of the fol-lowing strange circumstances ap-ply to you, maybe you can give the kid and the kitties a break.

You think a hearty "Meow" is the purr-fect alarm clock.

You always wanted a fur-decorated coat.

You're a frustrated hotel doorman.

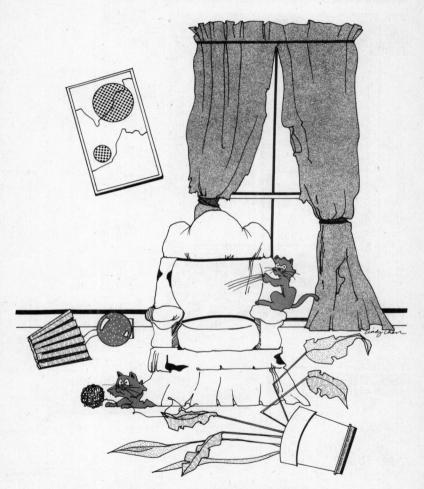

You want a home with that "lived-in" look.

You have won a lifetime supply of kitty litter.

You are tired of taking catnaps alone.

You know 3,028 ways to cook tuna.

You want an unusual centerpiece for those elegant soirées.

**You need a fresh scapegoat to absorb the blame for
misplaced car keys.**

Are You Cat Owner Material?

Okay, so you've decided you want to own a cat. Now the question is: Does the cat want to own you? As cats are increasingly the American pet of preference, more and more kitties can afford to be fussy.

A prospective bedmate wants to make sure you are real cat owner material and not some trendy type just picking up on the latest hip and furry status bauble.

Please answer the following questions, then wait. A kitty may call you—probably at about two in the morning.

1. When fixed with a penetrating stare, your inclination is to:
   (A) squirm.
   (B) call the police.
   (C) reach for the Amoré.

2. Your greatest health concern is:
   (A) high cholesterol.
   (B) low energy.
   (C) cold feet.

3. You have a burning passion to rid the world of:
   (A) war.
   (B) malnutrition.
   (C) fleas.

4. Your favorite antihero is:
   (A) Holden Caulfield.
   (B) Syd Vicious.
   (C) Garfield.

5. You like to collect:
   (A) rare stamps.
   (B) antique music boxes.
   (C) fur.

6. You believe a well-appointed house should have:
   (A) the newest appliances.
   (B) plenty of storage space.
   (C) custom-made mouse holes.

7. You enjoy waking up to:
(A) a Mozart sonata.
(B) seductive murmurs.
(C) whiskers and eyeballs.

8. In your opinion, the greatest scientific breakthrough of modern times is:
(A) the computer chip.
(B) laser technology.
(C) mint-scented kitty litter.

9. You sincerely believe that:
(A) E.T. will return.
(B) science will cure baldness.
(C) kitty will come when called.

10. The social cause most likely to win your support would be:
(A) amnesty for Zsa Zsa.
(B) prohibition of elevator music.
(C) national health insurance for pussycats.

11. You know the best way to get a cat to play with you is to:
(A) say "Let's play now, kitty."
(B) take a bath in catnip.
(C) start your income tax.

12. You know a cat is most likely to respond to the command "Stay" if she is:
(A) intelligent.
(B) cooperative.
(C) asleep.

13. As a newspaper reader you have developed the skill of:
(A) separating fact from fiction.
(B) evaluating sources.
(C) reading around a large mass of fur.

The Cat House

There are approximately seven zillion soft-focus photographs of cats in the world. Aesthetics aside, these pictures don't have much to do with the real animal scratching at your bedroom door.

What this means is that potential kitty owners aren't getting the real picture. They should not be expecting an animal whose main goal in life is to be sure the lighting is flattering. You can prove you are ready to care for a flesh-and-blood feline by deciding what's wrong with this picture. Then turn the page to confront the unvarnished truth.

Cat People vs. Dog People

The personal traits that differentiate dog people from cat people used to be predictable. Dog owners were Fortune 500 CEOs—tough, gruff guys who liked to give orders and kick butt. Cat owners were slightly asthmatic poets or spinsters or kids who took in occasional strays.

Today, however, the old stereotypes are gone and cat ownership is in. At this very moment, both Alexander Haig *and* Mia Farrow are likely to be stroking the furry chin of an Exotic Shorthair.

But if this isn't enough to persuade you that Americans everywhere are going cat-atonic over pussies, here are ten more reasons to own a cat rather than a dog.

1. You wish to remain on good terms with the mail carrier.

2. You would rather have a pet make sounds like Katharine Hepburn nuzzling with Spencer Tracy than like Sylvester Stallone taking on the Viet Cong.

3. If your animal is going to dig up the neighbor's pansy bed, you would at least like him to be slick enough not to get caught.

4. As both cats and dogs can smell bad, your choice is for the animal most likely to keep his distance.

5. Your definition of food does not include items purchased at Army surplus stores.

6. You do not believe it should be necessary to hire Barbara Wodehouse in order to instill in an animal the minimal principles of civilized conduct.

7. In your view, Mozart is not enhanced by an unrelenting accompaniment of high-pitched yelps and whimpers.

8. Realizing you can expect to live only seventy or so years, you are determined not to spend a good chunk of this time escorting an animal about the neighborhood aiding in his eternal search for the right tree against which to pee.

9. You respond more enthusiastically to affection when it is delivered by a tidy lick on the cheek rather than by a cupful of drool down the neck.

10. You believe your party guests are more charmed by a pet who naps on their coats than one who is obsessed with their crotches.

Typical Dog Person

Typical Cat Person

Cats vs. Kids: A Preliminary Survey

You're a Natural Cat Owner If . . .

- You prefer a creature smart enough not to need Pampers for the first three years of life.
- You don't want to "child-proof" your kitchen cabinets.
- You're looking forward to an adolescent who won't tie up the phone or beg to go to teeny bopper rock concerts.
- You don't want to live in fear of what those you raise will tell their therapists about you.
- You don't want to spend years answering the question "Why?"

CHAPTER 2
A Field Guide to Cats

Personality Types

"My Persian knows she is an objêt d'art. She always poses by the Chinese vase in the window," a purebred owner is likely to purr.

It's true, of course. The bigtime cat breeds do have their own idosyncratic ways—the "talkative" Siamese, the pixieish Havana Brown, and so forth.

But that isn't to say that the mangy mixed breeds the rest of us cuddle up with on cold winter nights don't have their own unique personalities. Here are just a few.

The Little Tramp

Her libido rises when the sun sets. She knows all the neighborhood toms by scent if not by name. Who asks? This isn't the Junior Cotillion.

She enjoys watching the toms hiss and claw their way to the front of the line every night as she feigns disinterest in them, licking an extra bit of sheen onto her tummy, a ritual that never fails to cause riots. In the end, however, she takes them all on anyway, the fat and gray, the lean and tan.

Sometimes after one of her owner's lectures on the difference between lust and love, the Little Tramp wonders about the emptiness of her encounters. Perhaps she should spend more time at home cuddling in her person's lap watching sitcoms. But then she glimpses her reflection in the mirror. Still a glamor puss, she assures herself, but the years are mounting. Even nine lives can be short, she reasons, and she has never been one to believe in a Big Cat House in The Sky.

So she opts to listen to her hormones instead and spends the day grooming herself in preparation for her moonlit encounters. Let her scaredy-cat sisters spend the wee hours warming feet. She'll go out and warm up the night.

The Little Tramp

The Playful Pussy

Every day at 6:17 A.M., the Playful Pussy breaks the sound barrier, fleeing an imaginary pit bull or chasing a phantom mouse around the house. At 6:18 he calls it quits. Until 6:19.

Then he begins to look for real stuff: a cashmere sweater to turn into something resembling a grade school art project, or a contraceptive device to deposit in the living room just as the dinner guests arrive.

Kick the Playful Pussy out, however, and you know where he is going to end up. He has been stuck in so many trees that the local fire department has named a ladder in his honor.

Some cat owners put up with all this craziness because they figure that the Playful Pussy will help them through those conversational dead spots with tedious visitors. But, as command performances are not the Playful Pussy's specialty, his single zany stunt, under these circumstances, will be to hibernate in the linen closet.

Kitty Plate

The Finicky Feline

When it comes to the mystery meat that passes for cat food these days, the Finicky Feline likes to quote Garfield: "The bouquet leaves something to be desired."

But this pussy's contempt for normal cat chow doesn't mean she is ready to stomach anything more exotic. At dinner time, she may whine with a persistence that rivals the Chinese water torture, but give her a piece of your meat loaf or prosciutto with melon and she'll dismiss the offering with a disdainful sniff.

The Finicky Feline makes more demands than Madonna on tour. But before you get too hard-nosed with this pussy, remember she can always move her show a few fences down the road, leaving you with no more than a catnip-scented toy mouse, a year's supply of mite preparation, and bittersweet memories of the food fights that you once shared.

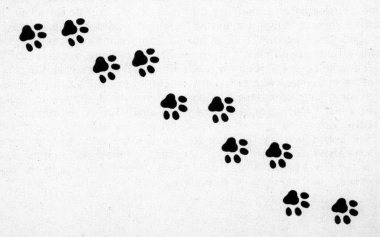

The Galloping Gourmand

It's dangerous to leave a science project unattended in the Galloping Gourmand's household. If it moves, he'll eat it. On the other hand, if it doesn't move, he'll eat it anyway.

Life is a bowlful of cherries for the G.G. Or a bowlful of sauerkraut. Or egg yolks. He's not fussy. Anything even remotely edible, from chicken gizzards to licorice cigars, can set his salivary glands to stirring.

He is the only cat in town with a double chin. When he gets up to walk, his belly stays on the floor. Recently your cousin embarrassed you by saying that your cat looked like a Marlon Brando with fur. But the Galloping Gourmand just purred sweetly as if to say, "Why, thank you. I'd love a piece of quiche."

And don't think this pudgy pussy is going to fall for any of those Soy Diet Delights. Try them and within a week you'll be visited by a delegation of irate neighbors with laundry lists of missing edibles ranging from boysenberry yogurt tarts to pet gerbils.

So until you can convince Dick Gregory to expand his operation to include fat cats, you'll just have to live with the Galloping Gourmand in whatever part of house and home he has not yet eaten you out of.

THE COOK

Pizza Palace of America · Food for a King

The Nervous Nellie

Just because she is paranoid does not mean no one is out to get her. The very existence of barking dogs and thunderclaps is reason enough for her to take up permanent residence under the bed.

Fleeing this safe haven because of some intruding vacuum cleaner hose or the presence of an old shoe that looks suspiciously alive, she will proceed to execute a six-foot standing high jump to escape whatever monsters have moved into the shag rug. If, however, she should chance to land on a bookshelf ledge, she will remember her fear of heights and nosedive back to earth.

During rare moments when she has nothing else to worry about, Nellie hangs around her food bowl wondering if she'll ever be fed again. When, in fact, she is, she won't bite right off but hesitates and paws the food, her eyes asking, "What's the catch?"

The Pampered Pet

Here we catch the Pampered Pet in a rare private moment, unaccompanied by her groomer, therapist, or astrologer. Sitting among silk and satin like the star performer in a Victorian brothel, she is indulged to a degree that would embarrass Leona Helmsley.

She owns a scratching post covered with custom-knotted mouse fur, but is as unlikely to recognize a real mouse as the Prince of Wales would be to identify the ingredients in a pig-knuckle-and-collard-green casserole.

It's not that her genes are crying out, "You will be miserable unless you are silver-spoon-fed slightly warmed portions of strained pheasant laced with truffles." It's just that no one gives her a lot of choice.

But the Pampered Pet doesn't complain. It takes a certain practiced aplomb to sit gracefully while someone rations out morsels of spiced duck liver—but it beats having to wonder about where your next meal is coming from.

The Couch Potato

He moves only to eat or change the channels. You'll get some idea of what his life is like if you submerge yourself in a pool of pillows, lower your eyelids to half-mast, and uncritically allow the sights and sounds of laugh track sitcoms, hyperactive weather people, and public TV pledge pitches to wash over you.

If the Couch Potato shows any preference, it's for steamy soap opera bedroom scenes. And then it's not so much the steam that attracts him as the bed.

How was this once-frisky kitty transformed into a lifeless lump? The unfortunate answer lies with his aggressively permissive owners, who have allowed their kitty to confuse liberty with license. First it was, "Well, okay, go ahead and watch the cat food commercials from the coffee table." Now it's degenerated to, "I wonder if you could spare *part* of the sofa on Super Bowl Sunday."

One kitty therapist recommended supervised exercise, but the Jane Fonda workout tape on the VCR only made ol' Couch Potato motion sick and caused him to throw up on the seat covers. Another professional suggested behavior modification—but how many slices of pepperoni pizza is one supposed to trade for a little space in one's own living room? The owners have decided that, oh, well, they never much liked that room anyway. They are talking with contractors about building an add-on—one without a cat door.

The Wild Cat

Though he may be in temporary captivity high above Park Avenue and East Fifty-third Street, he's planning to star in his own *National Geographic Special*—tracking unsuspecting ladybugs, ambushing the television set, and launching surprise attacks against brussels sprouts. Any goldfish or tweety bird that encroaches on his territory, however involuntarily, had better bring along a game warden.

At meal time, the Wild Cat's instincts crave fresh-caught gazelle flesh, but the Asphalt Jungle offers only Tender Vittles. Your best bet is to place some factory-made pet gruel behind the refrigerator, where the wild cat can actually hunt it down. He'll stalk his prey with fire in his eye, forgetting for the moment that the object of his quest is poultry by-products with sodium tripoly-phosphate added.

Do Cats Resemble Their Owners?

The answer, without pussyfooting around, is of course. As usual, Mother Goose had it right: There was a crooked man who bought a crooked cat. . . .

Without trying to deal with the larger question of just who in this mirror-image equation chooses whom, we present Exhibits A through F, some portraits of certain members of various cat breeds posing with their significant others.

The Persian Owner

The Abyssinian Owner

The Oriental Shorthair Owner

The American Shorthair Owner

The Bombay Owner

The Balinese Owner

Choosing a Name for Your Cat

Of course, as far as your cat is concerned, a "name" is an irrelevant concept. The only cats who respond to their names are those who have been brainwashed into thinking they are dogs. Still, owners are only human, and telling your Great Aunt Tillie how Oxydol got his name will deflect her questions about when you're going to meet some nice boy and settle down.

In other words, there's always a story behind a cat's name. Here are some of those stories.

Jimmy Smith, 10, Kid

My cat's name is S.P. It got that name because I found him when I was just two years old and some neighbor kids said I should name him Shitty Pants. I didn't know any better, so I did. But when my mom heard me call, "Here Shitty Pants, here Shitty Pants," she had a fit and said I couldn't call him that. I started to cry so my dad said, "Why not just call him S.P. for short?" so I did, and that's what he's been ever since.

Martin DiMartinez, 40, Bureaucrat

I call my cat Charlene because that was my first wife's name and *she* never listened to me either.

Heather Hill, 22, Video-Rental Clerk

My cat is named Moe. Originally I had three cats, but Curly ran off one day chasing an Egyptian Mau, and later Larry went to the big litter box in the sky, so now it's just us two stooges—me and Moe.

Julian Safire, 52, English Professor

I named my cats Who and Whom because everyone always gets them mixed up.

Tallulah Bernhardt, over 30, Waitress and Actress

I call my cat Sean Connery. I figure if I can't play opposite him at least I can play with him.

Sam Sneeky, 36, Tax Accountant

We named our cat Fido because our landlord hates cats but loves dogs. Fortunately, the landlord is nearsighted.

CHAPTER 3
A Field Guide to Cat Owners

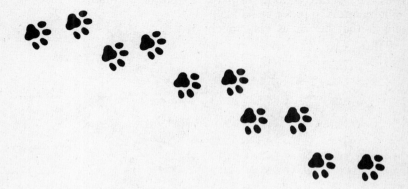

Types of Cat Owners

It is true, of course, that Richard Nixon's famous Checkers speech was not about a cat. We also know that Napoleon, who had this thing about undivided attention, couldn't seem to handle free-spirited felines.

But while we can make a good guess as to who *isn't* a cat person, we can never be so sure as to who the cat people are. Queen Victoria and Elizabeth Taylor have both loved kitties. So have Lincoln and Lenin, Sandy Dennis and Albert Schweitzer, and a lot of other people you would not want to invite to the same dinner party.

Nevertheless, order will be served by identifying some of the main species of the genus *cat owner*. While interbreeding between these types is possible, it is, at best, a dicey proposition.

Kid Owner

It's usually not difficult to identify the kid's cat. It's the one with the permanently tweaked tail and one ear stretched longer than the other. Some other kid will come by and see the cat sprawled in some weird position sleeping in the sun and want to know, "Is he dead?" The cat owner will deliver a karate chop to his pet's hindquarters to prove by half killing it that his cat is very much alive.

This is not to say the kid doesn't love his cat. He is proud of his kitty. There was the time he dropped him from the upstairs window to see if puss would really land on his feet. The next day he began selling tickets for a repeat performance, this time from the roof. His mother arrived just in time.

(Of course, some kids do not want to play spin the cat. Mature and sensitive children recognize that a cat is something other than a bundle of more or less movable parts. If you know a child with this kind of insight, you might get him to work on a problem worthy of his talents, like bringing peace to the Middle East.)

The Soft Touch

She keeps accumulating cats, clinging to the quixotic notion that someday, somehow, somewhere she'll find one who pays attention to her. She has even actually bought cats, rescuing them from the humiliation of equal billing with gerbils in pet store windows. Mostly, however, her cats just show up now that the word is out in cat hobo jungles all over America about the easy life at 195 South Elm Street in Akermanville, Idaho.

"How did you know you were meant for me, liddle puddy?" she will coo as she finds one more mangy specimen whining and clawing at her back door.

And then, of course, the Soft Touch acquires still more cats by ignoring an important natural law. Big pussies have little pussies, a rumor she considers blown

way out of proportion by the kitty-hating lunatic fringe.

When perfectly sane people ask her why she has so many cats the Soft Touch will describe the pleasure of watching fifteen cats scramble after the same scratching post or perching by the picture window in a lineup of furry backsides.

But she keeps the real reason to herself. She now has a houseful of companions, none of whom nag her to stop smoking, insist that she look at the bright side, or complain about ring around the collar.

The Competitor

You have a kitty. *She* has an Exhibit: a superior puss trained to endure while being stretched, poked, prodded, and trundled.

What this is all about, she will tell you, is "improving the breed," manufacturing an aristocratic kitty whose natural habitat is a purple velvet cushion in a lace-decorated wire cage no bigger than a bread box.

If ordinary cat-owning mortals can't fathom the Competitor's obsession with creating a Platonic Japanese Bobtail, well, the Competitor understands their limitation. She herself remembers what it was like before cat contests became her religion: how she once believed that cats were meant to pursue mice rather than rosette ribbons and kitschy gold-plated trophies; how she was driven from her first cat show by a stench so strong it could only have been emanating from a litter box the size of Detroit; how her idea of a "flawed" cat used to be one with an eye missing or a big hunk chewed out of its tail.

Now, however, her trained eye recognizes right off the sad handicap of a Siamese with a break in its whiskers or an Egyptian Mau whose green eyes are not the required gooseberry green. Her cat show wardrobe includes colors ranging from white to ivory to accommodate the flurry of flying dusting powder.

But after the last judge has spoken and she returns home with her puss who, it turns out, had too many spots in all the wrong places, the Competitor becomes a cat lover just like you and me, wondering if this is the night her kitty will allow a little gentle stroking. Once she's alone, pussy one-up-manship is no longer her obsession. She knows there is no guarantee that the cover kitty on *Cat World* magazine would be any good at all at the important stuff like keeping her feet warm on cold February nights.

The Cat-a-holic

It's difficult to know which she loves more: her cats or her cat kitsch.

She owns enough kitty-shaped porcelain Christmas ornaments to decorate the tree at Rockefeller Center. She has cat calendars dating back to 1941, as well as the largest collection of cat T-shirts and cat earrings in town. Her notion of an elegantly appointed living room includes a multi-level cat climbing tower as a focal point.

When she is not dusting, polishing, or otherwise embellishing her cat collectibles, the Cat-a-holic likes to regale friends and co-workers with tales of her real-life pussies' remarkable achievements. Toby recently began flicking off the light switch to cut back on electricity, while Jezebel waltzes around the bedroom choreographing *Swan Lake*.

If listeners sometimes respond to her accounts of these feline feats with skepticism—"Has anyone actually *seen* your cat use toilet paper?" a rude coworker asked recently—she brushes aside the comment. Why should she worry about the bad manners of people who would rather ramble on about growth stocks and undiscovered restaurants than watch kitty kicking a raisin around the living room?

She does believe, however, that if they could share her experience as she returns home from a reluctant weekend away from her cat-shaped garbage can, her Laurel Burch cat sheets, and, of course, her cats, to be told by the sitter that the pets were miserable in her absence, her friends and associates, too, might understand the true joys of owning a pussy.

The Black-Cat Owner

The Black-Cat Owner won't be volunteering as community outreach chairman at the Junior League. She knows that collecting Toys for Tots would ruin her image.

For her, kitty is a lifestyle appendage, like her all-black wardrobe and black jewelry from Tanzania. The black cat, the white walls, the paintings by a Jackson Pollack imitator—this woman is a long way from Laura Ashley.

If the Black-Cat Owner is less intrigued by her puss than other cat owners are by theirs, it could be because—well, in a way, she *herself* is a cat. Like her cat, she works at being a mystery, purring languidly through half-closed eyes, inspiring thoughts of jet-set trysts and Swiss bank accounts. The Black-Cat Owner will not be found at the local A & P exchanging discount coupons for Meow Mix.

Like her cat, she refuses to come when you call, and she doesn't remember your birthday. And like all cats, she expects you to pick up the dinner check while she, felinelike, picks at the salmon mousse.

In short, the Black-Cat Owner wants you to believe that she, like her pussy, is introverted, devious, and self-centered. Some good advice: take her word for it.

The Reluctant Cat Owner

He's the type who has never been able to understand why anyone would want to gum up a perfectly good coffee mug with some pictures of a grinning feline. And this blind spot has caused the reluctant cat owner a few problems in his social life.

During his single days he would often notice that the most desirable women owned the most obnoxious cats. But there came a time that the desire became overwhelming and he married one of the women and, in the bargain, her feline.

Unfortunately his feeling toward kitty has not really mellowed over time. On days when he finds paw prints on the hood just after he has washed the car, he is capable of mentally engineering the cat's demise. Why not, for instance, quicksand in the litter box? Who would notice until it was too late?

But instead of escalating violence, he and the cat have settled for a reciprocal disdain. "Your cat wants in," he'll say several times an evening, never budging.

Sometimes on those mornings when the cat claws the sports page into confetti before he's had a chance to read it, he will rehearse an ultimatum. "Either the cat goes or I go." But as he knows his wife would not find this a particularly difficult choice, he keeps his mouth shut.

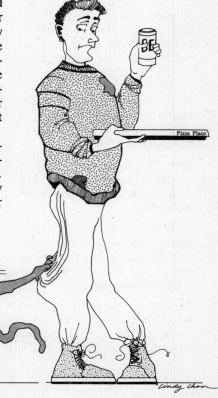

What Kind of Cat Owner Are You?

Cat people are getting organized. Just plain old "cat owner" these days isn't enough. The pressure is on for you to be a dues-paying "Lover" or a card-carrying "Fancier." Capital L. Capital F.

The problem with this trend is that most cat people, like their pussies, are individualists. They want to be free to either coax their cat in at night or to throw him out, to give as much attention to kitty's astrological chart as to his shot record, or to lend him to friends with mice problems.

So go ahead. Express yourself. Cat ownership can be an art form. Here's some help figuring out your cat-raising style.

Realistic. I have decorated any space my cat might invade in the style of YMCA locker room, circa 1950.

Hip, New Age. The emergency phone number of my cat's acupuncturist is listed on his name tag.

Aesthetic. When I am entertaining, my mauve-and-tan cats are trained to position themselves on the peaches-and-cream chaise lounge.

Shameless. I do not blush when the men from Goodwill come to pick up a cat-mauled sofa that I am claiming is in good condition so I can take the deduction on my income tax.

Touchy/Feely. When, on entering the shower stall, I step in a pile of cat crap, I reflect that my puss must be acting out feelings brought on by a bout of low self-esteem.

Practical. I have no trouble training my cats. I figure out what they like to do and then tell them to do it.

Occult. I take the overturned lamp I return to at the end of each day to be the work of a poltergeist—*not* my kitty.

Defensive. When a guest shows up who is allergic to cats, I am torn between locking the cat or the guest in the bathroom.

A Return to the Great "Cats vs. Kids" Debate

The social philosophers are wringing their hands—civilization, they say, has reached a point at which cat food gets more attention than baby gruel.

But it's time to tell the pontificators to lighten up. "Cats or kids" is still very much an open question, despite the high cost of sneakers. Cooler heads have compiled some objective arguments on both sides of the debate.

In Favor of Kids

When a kid dissects a mouse, he does it in science class.

No cat will ever give you a World's Best Mom cup.

Kids make less noise when grounded and in heat.

A kid won't spray after two years.

You can't threaten a cat with no dessert.

In Favor of Cats

Cats don't need new shoes every six months.

You can't take off and leave your kid with a bowlful of Tender Vittles and a catnip mouse.

Kids are unreliable mousers.

A dumb cat is no reflection on your personal pedigree.

You don't have to worry when your cat stays out till 3 A.M.

CHAPTER 4
Getting to Know Kitty

The Cat Owner's *Webster's*

It's no secret that cat owners share a language all their own. At home, it's the corny stuff: "How's my itty-bitty kitty?" At cat shows it's got a competitive edge: "My Monique has a more perfect colorpoint pattern than those other mangy beasts."

But there's a lot more to cat talk than trite run-of-the-mill endearments and cat show one-upmanship. Here, published for the first time, is *Webster's Cat's Unabridged Dictionary.*

Alley cats. Macho and promiscuous cats now becoming obsolete, thanks to cat-neutering clinics and the spread of alleyless suburbs.

Castration. A population-control operation favored by all members of the cat community except cats.

Cat allergy. Acceptable excuse for the reclusive socially inept.

Cat courtship. A prelude to cat sex, typically measured in milliseconds.

Cat door. Monument to cat indecision. Opens and closes more often than the entrance to Bloomingdale's on Christmas Eve.

Cat I.Q. test. Examination the truly smart cat is clever enough to dodge.

Cat show. The only type of beauty contest in which the judges are allowed to poke, pat, and stroke the contestants in public.

Catnip. The dry martini of the cat world but without the liver problems.

Claws. Appendages that, while limiting a cat's ability to perform Chopin, are considerably more help than mere fingers in unraveling the rug.

Exercise. Fitness regimen undertaken by cats only at 4:47 A.M. in your bedroom.

Flea. Cat's contribution to the summertime parade of unwanted houseguests.

Fur ball. Small, unpleasant cat-to-owner present usually deposited on the Oriental rug with great drama during the annual Invite-the-Boss-Home-to-Dinner festivities.

Litter box. Receptacle for cat poo that comes, regardless of dimensions, in only one size: too small.

Meow. All purpose cat word that can be translated variously to mean "Give me" or "No way."

Mommy's Precious. How Aunt Sylvia refers to her obnoxious cat Stinkums, who's not nearly as sweet as your own Buster.

Mouse. Once-endangered species now in plentiful supply, thanks to Fancy Feast.

Pedigree papers. Costly documents that are often the only way to tell the deluxe model cat from the no-frills variety.

Scratching post. Cat word for sofa (or sweater; or stockings).

Spray. Cat graffiti with no paint necessary.

Tail. Appendange that helps distinguish a cat from a meat loaf.

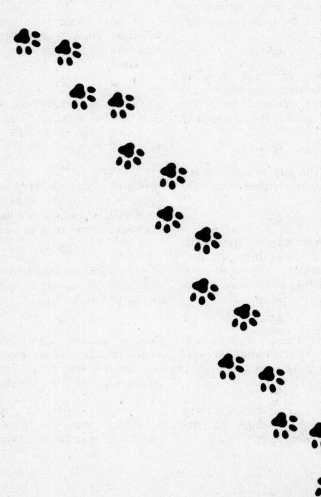

Dear Tabby (Letters to Tabby van Buren)

Some misguided cat owners are actually *amused* by their cat's problems. When a neurotic puss takes up permanent residence inside an A & P bag, these sad cases aren't concerned, merely diverted. "Oh, look. Isn't that cute?" they'll purr.

Fortunately, most cat owners want to do what they can to help their kitties work through problems. That's why they seek the advice of Dear Tabby, the only cat-behavior expert who behaves like a cat—because she *is* one. Here's just a sampling from Dear Tabby's latest collection.

Dear Tabby,

I have been trying to get my cat Jonah to pose in a Santa Claus hat and whiskers for a Christmas Card, but he always runs away. Tabby, Jonah is so cute he would make a perfect Christmas greeting. Every year I get a card from my sister-in-law with a picture of her dumb dog dressed in a Santa outfit. He's panting and drooling and nowhere near as good-looking as my Jonah.

But no matter how much I flatter Jonah, no matter how much I beg, whenever I bring out the Santa hat and beard, he hisses and runs away. What can I do to get Jonah to sit still and smile for a Christmas portrait?

Signed, Frustrated in Philadelphia

Dear Frustrated,

Has it ever occurred to you that Jonah may be Jewish?

Dear Tabby,

I'd like to think my cat loves all of me, but he seems particularly enamored of my toes, nose, and earlobes. My problem is, Tabby, that attention to these spots tickles. What can I do?

Signed, A Sensitive Gal in St. Louis

Dear Sensitive,

Your problem, unfortunately, is common, and only one thing seems to work. Wear Hush Puppies, earmuffs, and a nose guard, and stay out of polite company.

Dear Tabby,

My cat overeats, oversleeps, and underexercises, to say nothing of what he is up to between midnight and 4:30 A.M. every night. My question is, Tabby, what do I have to do to get a job like this?

Signed, Sick and Tired in Cincinnati

Dear Sick,

It's a long shot, but consider reincarnation.

Dear Tabby,

My cat Muffin has had a fetish for the Do Not Remove Under Penalty of Law tag on my pillow. Now she has completely demolished it and I find myself lying awake at night worrying: Will my pussy be arrested?

Signed, Worried in Waukegan

Dear Worried,

What a cat-astrophe. Muffin should turn herself in immediately to the Pillow Protection Agency and hope that the judge who tries the case is a pussycat.

Dear Tabby,

My cat Attila not only nuzzles up to mice, his best friend in the world is our pet canary. Tabby, people are laughing at us. Should we get Attila some assertiveness training?

Signed Embarrassed in Easthampton

Dear Embarrassed,

I don't think so. Attila deserves your congratulations for breaking out of the stereotypes that still restrict so many of our kitties today. Rather than being pushed into assertiveness training, Attila should be encouraged to join a group of like-minded pets in the Caring Cat Movement who understand that for the modern cat bonding is in, macho is out.

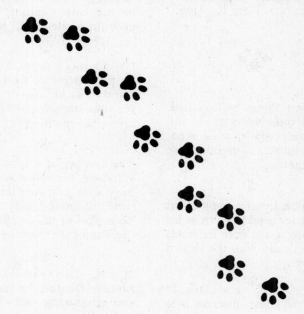

Penetrating the Cat Mystique

First off, let's admit there is too much fast-and-loose generalizing about cats. *Your* cat may be lazy and aloof. That does not mean *mine* cannot be energetic and affectionate.

The Great Cat Maker in the Sky has allowed room for a lot of cat quirkiness. Yet He or She wants us to be able to recognize a cat when we encounter one. Hence, the Architect of the Grand Scheme of Things has established certain immutable laws of cat behavior. Here they are.

All other things being equal, a cat's immediate needs will be served only by what is behind a bookcase or otherwise unreachable.

The intensity of a cat's effort to transfer used litter from his litter box to the floor increases geometrically with the size of the box.

A cat will lose interest in a new toy approximately fifteen seconds after he has battered it to the point at which it cannot be returned to the store.

The more nervous the person asking "Does he scratch?" the more likely the cat will be to provide a quick answer.

The day the cat owner comes to understand that the cat wants only the creamy part of the Oreo is the day the cat will decide to eat the cookie and pass up the cream.

The more expensive the cat's sleeping basket the greater will be the cat's naptime preference for a pile of old socks.

On entering a room, a cat will be most attracted to that person who would most prefer to see him stuffed and mounted above the mantelpiece.

The number of rooms a dedicated cat can strew with garbage after an owner leaves for work is limited only by the floor plan of the dwelling and the size of the wastebasket.

If your five-year-old brings home Dexter, a skinny, starved-looking cat who was "abandoned in the park," the odds are that "Dexter" will give birth to a litter of six next week.

The greater the cat owner's need to withdraw into his own thoughts, the greater his cat's motivation to pounce on him from the recesses of some dark closet.

A cat's motivation to uncover some half-rotting delicacy in the garbage can increases proportionately the closer said morsel is to the bottom of the container.

A cat's prompt response to an owner's instruction can be directly correlated to what the cat intended to do anyway.

The cat owner's Bitter Truth: Your cat is attracted to the following stimuli in descending order. 1-His food. 2-Other cats. 3-Dogs. 4-Any of a thousand or so curious inanimate objects. 5-You.

All cats are *always* on the wrong side of the door.

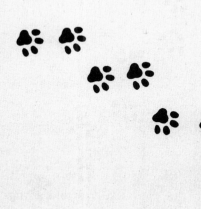

The Cat's Daily Planner

If you think your cat spends all day sleeping, yawning, and eating, you haven't been paying attention.

Pusses of the 1990s lead fuller lives than their ancestors. After all, they've grown up with *Sesame Street,* the Yuppie movement, and 237,000 personal self-help books telling how to find fulfillment.

This preoccupation with quality time hasn't been lost on the kitties of the world, all the half-closed eyes and selective deafness notwithstanding. Indeed, if your pet doesn't already have a personal daily planner, chances are he will soon. It will probably look something like this.

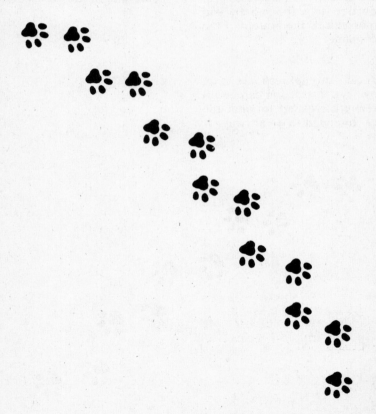

5:45 Wake owner for breakfast

6:00 Reject Seafood Supper as not proper breakfast. Find old pork chop behind couch. Eat for breakfast

7:00–7:15 Rearrange self in A & P bag

7:15–7:45 Stare at Bryan Gumbel

7:45–9:00 Snooze in underwear drawer

9:00–9:03 Chase tail

9:04–10:00 Nap on pile of clean laundry

10:00–10:05 Demolish heirloom needlepoint footstool

10:05–10:10 Discover old fig behind stove, chase around house until covered with grime; eat

10:10–12 noon Find new pile of clean laundry; take nap on it

Noon Regard lunch, walk away

12:01 Munch on houseplant

12:05 Start bath

12:10 Cut bath short to begin afternoon nap promptly; sprawl out on stairs; ignore people tripping; dream about herding mice and shredding toilet paper

4:10 Wake up and shred toilet paper

4:18 Recline on Chippendale chair long enough to make daily hair deposit

4:30 Optional staring time

4:50 Locate unscratched table leg (if any); scratch

4:55 Begin evening mealtime ritual; nuzzle cook; meow; whine; block access to stove; wind self around ankles of cook; continue until cook offers sample of coq au vin

5:30 Reject sample; not enough vin

6:00 Stare at diners during meal; look sad and skinny; yowl

7:00 Sleep on TV with tail dangling in front of screen

8:00 Wake up for cat food commercial; meow, whimper, and whine

8:01 Return to sleeping position

9:14 Keep urgent appointment with invisible object in the foyer

10:00 Report for nightly foot-warming duties

A Cat's-Eye View of the World

Even with the rapid kitty progress of recent years, there are, unfortunately, still no cat movie directors. When one does come along to show us what a cat's life is really like, we can be sure it will not be through the camera eye of a six-foot Homo sapiens.

With cats, it's mostly high angles and low angles, depending on whether the pussy is scrunching into a rug, looking up, or perched on a ceiling beam looking down.

Until the first feline Woody Allen comes along, this cat photo collection will have to suffice to give you some idea of how cats see the world.

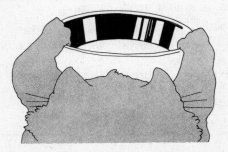

Yo, over here. I'm a party animal.

The time I was left high and dry.

As every cat knows, old chewing gum never dies.
It just hangs there.

So what's this about cats smelling up the house?

Okay, he's no Robert Redford. He keeps me in Kal Kan.

I call this one "Study in Frustration."

The day my outing took a wrong turn.

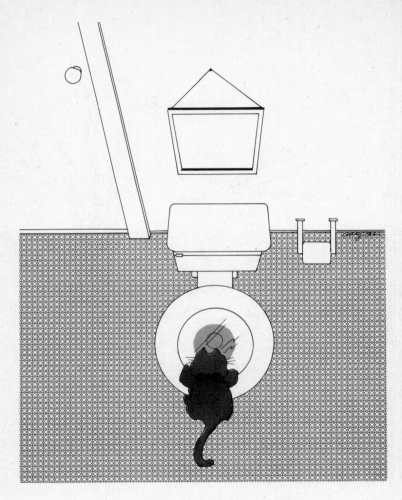

It's not Perrier, but it's always there.

**Some people never
appreciate your gifts.**

Your Relationship with Your Cat

Building a strong relationship with your cat requires patience and purr-sistence. As in any give-and-take relationship (mostly you give, puss takes), there are bound to be a few snags (on the drapes, the chairs, your stockings).

This special report, based on the popular best-seller *No More Pussyfooting Around,* tells how to build and maintain a healthy relationship with your puss.

You and Your Cat: A Relationship Guide for the 90s

Has your pussy begun to snub you in favor of a pile of old socks? Is he leaving unattractive kitty deposits in unusual places? Does he disappear for days on end and then come home looking like something the cat dragged in?

If so, you are not alone. Even in the most ideal person/pussy relationships, including some you may have seen featured in *Good Catkeeping* magazine, the fur occasionally flies.

Studies by cat psychologists tell us that up to 80 percent of person/pussy relationships undergo occasional strain, a whopping 50 percent experience severe estrangement, and in an unfortunate 20 percent, the parties are unable to resolve their differences, and break up.

Whether your pussy is peevish because you are working overtime or has just inexplicably begun to treat you like part of the furniture, this article offers tips from some of the country's top kitty mental health experts on how to cope.

Of course, you have the option of calling in a cat psychologist, but if you do, be sure to shop around to ensure that you find a reputable professional. Pussy psychology, like every field, has its bad apples, and you don't want to pay eighty dollars an hour just to have someone tell you that when your cat tears up your pantyhose he isn't really being mean, he is merely demonstrating his individuality. A good dedicated professional will give you step-by-step instructions for turning a cat-astrophic relationship into one that's the cat's pajamas.

One question inevitably arises in person/pussy relationships on the skids: Who is to blame? In pussy's eyes, there is seldom any doubt. Suppose, after years of cuddling up with kitty after dinner to watch the nighttime soaps, you suddenly begin serving candlelit dinners to a stranger. Any kitty worth his catnip, of course, knows how unhealthy it is to hold in pussy feelings. So he puts a paw in the soup just as the stranger nuzzles your foot beneath the table during dinner. Or he has an "accident" on the stranger's leg during an even more intimate moment.

Your reaction to the problem, of course, is different—something more along the lines of a quick look at your copy of *101 Uses for a Dead Cat*. Nonetheless, the sad fact remains: Pussy/person relationships in 1990 still reflect values forged before the Pussy Owner Liberation Movement. It will be wise to remember, thus, that your kitty's attitudes and responses were learned during less enlightened times. That means it will probably be easier to modify your own behavior than to ask kitty to modify his.

Relationship expert Madeline Manx advises allowing kitty to play a role in new endeavors, be they romances, hobbies, or new jobs. "I'm not suggesting a ménage à trois with your pet," she laughs. "I'm just saying that kitty needs more attention when something else new is going on in the house. Cats like to think they're the whole kitten caboodle."

Suppose your relationship problem with your puss is just the opposite? More and more you find yourself relying on kitty as a companion. "There is nothing wrong with allowing a cat to be your significant other," says Penelope Persian, director of the Cat House, a nonprofit Chicago-based cat behavior institute.

Cats can be ideal companions because they're so democratic, says Persian. "They don't care if you're Linda Evans or some slob with a rotten personality in the Bronx who is always putting his foot in his mouth. Oh, dear, I hope you don't print that."

But sometimes, of course, reliance on kitty can go too far. If you find yourself asking your cat to remind you to buy more beer, it is probably time to reassess your relationship with your pet. You don't want your relationship with your pussy to become clawstrophobic.

What Your Cat Is Trying to Tell You

Modern cat owners find themselves permanently in debt to the pioneer cat observer Jules Champfleury, who seemed to have enough time on his hands to record sixty-three variations of cat "meow."

Unfortunately, however, the great man did not answer the question so vital to kitty–person communications: What do these mumblings *mean*? Which are saying "yech," "barf," and "buzz off"? Which are saying "hello there," "move over," and "not too bad"?

Now, however, new research focusing on kitty body language is opening a new era that, when it comes to communicating with pussies, promises to turn modern cat owners into veritable Dr. Dolittles. Among the most recent findings:

What cat does	What cat means
Stares blankly when you ask which of three pairs of panty hose best matches your dress.	I'm a garter belt pussy myself.
Knocks over lamp while you read the sports page.	Remember me?
Jumps at unseen object.	We are not alone.
Stretches out after spaying.	Don't get around much anymore.
For the first time in months climbs on your lap and snuggles.	You're not going to let a little thing like that turkey breast I just ate come between us, are you?
Whines every week when you tune in *Dynasty*.	Can't we watch *Wonderful World of Animals* once in a while?
Stretches paws, arches back, and jumps up and down.	"I love your Jane Fonda workout tape."
Dramatically barfs up medicine you have secretly mixed with cat food.	"If you want a dumb animal, get a dog."
Yawns dramatically.	It's the company, not the hour.
Starts clawing at phone cord while you talk.	It's time to reach out and touch someone furry.

The Cat's Lexicon and Phrase Book

What he says	What he means
"Meow."	"Feed me."
"Merr-oow."	"*Please* feed me."
"MA-ROW."	"Feed me—NOW."
"Murf."	"I'd like it ever so much if you'd just feed me."
"Nak."	"Feed me something else."
"Pur-r-r"	"Maybe if I'm nice you'll feed me."

CHAPTER 5
Life With Kitty

The Kitty I.Q. Test

When it comes to impressing you with their intellects, most cats like to play the same mind game that many humans have also mastered. It goes: Now I'm looking at you very intently. Therefore I must be some kind of genius.

Don't be fooled. Sure, unlike a dog, many cats are smart enough to know that an automobile tire rotating at sixty miles an hour is dangerous and not particularly good to eat. On the other hand, most certified Mensa members of any species are not content to spend entire mornings licking The Right Spot.

The only way to tell how your cat really stacks up in the I.Q. rat race is to try her out on the following Kitty I.Q. Test. We supply no interpretation of the answers, so you will be able to judge your kitty's I.Q. in the context of any misconceptions, warped impressions, and outright delusions you have a need to hold on to.

1. Your cat makes use of the toilet to:
(A) fall into.
(B) crap.
(C) read.

2. When your cat sees another cat on TV, she:
(A) yawns.
(B) meows.
(C) changes the channel.

3. When you unpack the tuna from the grocery bag, your cat:
(A) stares.
(B) licks his chops.
(C) runs for the can opener.

4. When the doorbell rings, your cat:
(A) sleeps.
(B) peeks out.
(C) checks her makeup.

5. When you serve your cat food he does not like, he:
(A) leaves it.
(B) sits on it.
(C) threatens to report you to the SPCA.

6. When your cat is in a good mood he:
(A) rubs your leg.
(B) whistles.
(C) tells jokes.

7. When your cat hears music on the radio, he:
(A) hides.
(B) rocks and rolls.
(C) calls in a request.

8. When your cat finds a ball of yarn, she:
(A) jumps.
(B) juggles it.
(C) knits booties for the grandkittens.

9. When your cat travels in the car he:
(A) yowls.
(B) navigates.
(C) drives.

10. When your cat talks, she uses:
  (A) a basic meow.
  (B) meow with gestures.
  (C) French.

11. When a dog barks, your cat:
  (A) runs.
  (B) dials 911.
  (C) harmonizes in perfect thirds.

The Care and Feeding of Your Cat

Raising a kitty, you will find, brings certain tense moments when you and your animal cannot ignore the fact that you live under the same roof. You must deal with each other up close and personal.

Such moments need cause you no special anxiety. All you need do is surrender unconditionally and abjectly to whatever your puss has in mind.

However, as some stiff-necked incorrigibles are unwilling to accept such a peaceable solution and seem instead to live for nasty confrontation, here is a step-by-step guide to irritating the hell out of your pussy.

Dealing with Fleas

1. Sneak flea product into house during dead of night.

2. Stock up on Band-Aids.

3. Block all escape routes.

4. Hide flea remover inside shirt.

5. Put on hockey mask and gloves.

6. Open can of tuna fish to attract cat.

7. Pounce on cat.

8. Stroke, whisper endearments, and otherwise conceal real motives.

9. Dump flea product on cat. Ignore fleas jumping onto shirt.

9. Keep brush in general vicinity of squirming cat.

10. Continue until wounds get nasty or cat escapes.

11. If first treatment is ineffective, apply product again.

12. If second treatment is ineffective, train fleas and open flea circus.

"Morris, Time for Din-din. . . ."

1. Buy large economy-size bag of cat food with bonus plastic kitty dish.

2. Put out food in bonus dish.

3. Wait.

4. Wait more.

5. Throw out bag of cat food. Buy canned variety. Put out in plastic dish.

6. Wait

7. Buy new kitty dish with cat's name engraved on it. Put out canned cat food in new dish.

8. Wait.

9. Throw out canned cat food.

10. Buy butcher-prepared cat food. Put out food in name-engraved dish.

11. Wait.

12. Buy silver kitty dish. Put out butcher-prepared cat food in silver kitty dish.

13. Wait.

14. Throw out butcher-prepared cat food. Prepare homemade cat food and put in silver kitty dish.

15. Wait.

16. Throw out homemade cat food.

17. Throw out cat.

Giving Your Cat the Very Expensive Medication That the Vet Just Prescribed

1. Pay outrageous price for cat medication.

2. Tell cat you have something to make him feel better. Get out bottle and spoon.

3. Retrieve cat from neighbor's roof.

4. Wrap cat securely in towel.

5. Force open cat mouth and jam in medication.

6. Wipe medication off wall.

7. Buy more medication.

8. Rewrap cat in towel. Get out spoon.

9. Dispose of shredded towel.

10. Get bright idea. Put medication in cat food.

11. Wipe cat food plus medication off wall.

12. Decide cat is looking better.

Teaching Your Old Cat New Tricks: How to Roll Over

Day 1

1. Cancel all engagements indefinitely.
2. Stock up on tidbits.
3. Demonstrate process. Get down on floor and roll over. Ignore severe pinch in sacroiliac.
4. Smile at cat, give self tidbit, and say yum-yum.
5. Make sure no one is listening and say to cat, "Kitty wanna roll over? Get tidbit? Yum-yum?"
6. Translate cat stare to mean wild enthusiasm.
7. Tackle cat and roll cat over. Ignore severe scratch on forearm.
8. Repeat process until you, cat, or tidbits are exhausted.

Days 2–37

Repeat lesson, building on what cat has retained from previous day. Buy journal to record cat's progress.

Day 38

Realize cat is too smart to waste time doing stupid pet tricks. Convert blank journal to recipe book.

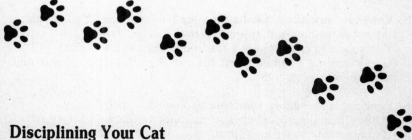

Disciplining Your Cat

Whoever invented the title Animal Control Officer hadn't spent much time around cats. Time spent trying to control your cat is about as productive as time spent collecting string.

But lately, cat misbehavior experts have developed new schemes for making kitty paw the line—schemes that promise a solution until someone is foolhardy enough to try one.

In the quiz below, test your knowledge of these new discipline techniques.

1. Your cat devours every house plant you bring home. You should:
(A) appeal to cat's aesthetic sense. Buy tacky plastic plants.
(B) start a collection of prickly pear cactus plants.
(C) buy your next plant at the Little Shop of Horrors.

2. Your cat spits and hisses whenever you try to bathe him. You should:
(A) buy a spittoon.
(B) hiss and spit back.
(C) mellow him out. Spike his cat nip with a dollop of Four Roses.

3. Your cat gloms on to the drapes with a death grip whenever you bring out the cat carrier. You should:
(A) find a vet who makes house calls.
(B) equip the carrier with stereophonic mouse sounds and posters of the Play Pussy of the Month.
(C) buy a cat carrier large enough to hold a cat and a drape.

4. Your cat regularly pees in your new husband's shoes. You should:
(A) lock in closet (shoes, not cat or husband).
(B) throw away shoes and move to southern California beach community.
(C) reconsider old husband.

5. Your cat "mistakes" the bathtub for his litter box. You should:
(A) put litter box in bathtub and take sponge baths.
(B) explain to cat it's only a few more steps to the toilet.
(C) violate cat's innate need for privacy. Rent out rooms and increase bathroom traffic.

6. Your cat is shredding your couch. You should:
(A) buy matching couches labeled yours and mine.
(B) redecorate in wrought iron.
(C) leave out pamphlets with titles like "Declawing for Beginners."

7. Your cat won't eat. You should:
(A) carve out mouse-shaped entrées.
(B) serve the kitty drinks before dinner.
(C) put cat food dinner on family dinner plates and wait for the inevitable.

8. You are tired of watching your cat violate your lessons on proper cat behavior. You should:

(A) reason with him.
(B) make threats.
(C) not look.

The Petersons' Top-Secret Tips for Giving Away a Litter

As the most dedicated pussy lover knows, even the cutest kitten grows up to be a cat.

As a better-educated public becomes increasingly aware of this inevitable metamorphosis, it gets harder all the time to pass off kitties, cute as they might be when three weeks old.

Here are some truly desperate suggestions for getting rid of the little buggers.

1. Give out kittens as Halloween treats.

2. Mail them in packages labeled "You have already won."

3. Start a rumor that mice are invading the neighborhood.

4. Announce to well-oiled cocktail party guests that they may take home the "pretty itty kitties."

5. Have a plane fly over the Super Bowl towing a banner asking "Anyone want a kitty?"

6. Surprise teacher with free kittens at local school on show-and-tell day.

7. Mail to friends and neighbors copy of article from *Good Housekeeping:* "How My Cat Saved Our Marriage."

8. Donate surprise gift boxes to annual church raffle, being sure to conceal air holes.

9. Start a "Save Our Kitties" Foundation and place heart-warming adoption ads directed to the Volvo set in highbrow magazines.

10. Put on doorstep of local humanitarian, ring bell, and run like hell.

Sensitivity Training for Cat Owners

It is important to keep in mind that you are not a cat. Sure, like your cat, you may lick your dinner plate when you've missed lunch, space out when you're bored, and pass up a meal altogether to make love. But when you are pregnant, you are not always able to seek out a secluded place for a gestation period. On the other hand, when your cat is pregnant, she is not about to take a Lamaze class and insist that the father be around for the birthing experience.

Despite such differences, you may benefit from time to time by putting yourself in your kitty's paws. Try the following sensitizing experiences.

1. Sprawl across the bed for a nap. Just as you doze off, have someone pick you up and dump you on the floor.

2. Discipline yourself to stare for hours at the pendulum of a grandfather clock while wearing a look that says, "One false move, Clock, and you've had it."

3. Go out in the yard and hunt relentlessly all morning for a garter snake. Kill it. Bring the snake in and place it on your housemate's lap. Suffer in silence as your housemate screams and flushes the snake down the garbage disposal.

4. On a night when you are starving, have someone serve you a heaping plateful of turnips, which you hate. Have the waiter tell you there's nothing else on the menu.

5. Frolic with a piece of cellophane. Thrill to the music of the crackles and the crinkles. As you prepare to explore the mystery further, stand helplessly by while a large vacuum cleaner comes along and sucks up your treasure.

6. Take an excessive interest in a fly on the window. Bat at the fly frenetically all afternoon, trying to perfect aim, unaware that there are always two sides to every window.

7. Have your sex life restricted to only lovers whose pedigrees have been verified by a committee of which you are not a member.

8. Spend a weekend stuck at home alone with a bowlful of food and a squeaky toy while everyone else in the house takes off for Lake Berryessa.

9. Confine your explorations into the outside world to what you can see through the air holes of a carrying box.

10. Next time you go in for a complete physical, allow the doctor to pick you up by the scruff and look you over.

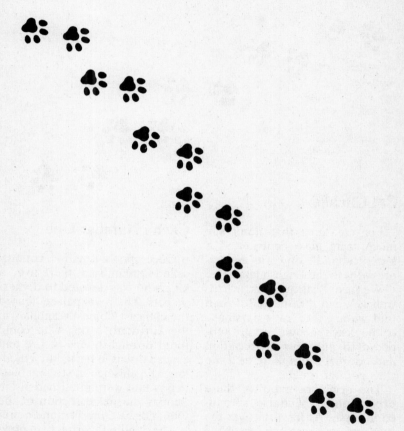

CHAPTER 6
The Cultural Cat

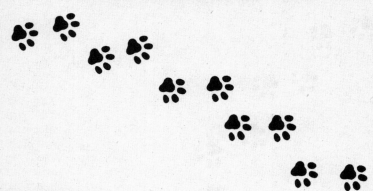

Cat Clichés

For creatures that don't say much, cats have contributed a kitten caboodle of words and expressions to the English language.

We have "cat burglars," "catwalks," and "catnaps." When told we are the "cat's pajamas" or the "cat's meow," we are supposed to purr our appreciation and not just stand there as if the cat's got our tongue.

The origin of many of these expressions is, of course, shrouded in myth. At least this was the case until our researchers started rooting about in the litter box of etymological history to come up with the True Stories behind some of the great cat clichés. Here they are.

Cliché Number One

Once upon a time in a country called Outlandisha, there lived a king who was devoted to domestic pets. The royal palace housed the choicest domestic animals in the kingdom: a dog who could jump through hoops of fire and catch a discus in his teeth; a monkey who chiseled in stone tablets essays that were published in the Sunday magazine section of the Outlandisha *Observer*; and more.

The king's favorite pet, however, was Archimedes, an Abyssinian cat who was so intelligent he had learned to play "Clair de Lune" on the royal lute.

One day, much to the king's

dismay, a hit-and-run chariot struck Archimedes, who henceforth suffered from amnesia. The pet forgot not only how to play the lute but how to lap up royal milk.

The king was so distraught he dedicated himself to restoring Archimedes' memory, but the royal court became alarmed as the king grew increasingly remote, eventually refusing to talk at all. The queen, outraged and jealous, gave the king an ultimatum: either he took a course in marital communications or she would enroll in real castle school, get her license, and leave. At this the king confessed, speaking thickly, that one day he had knelt down at Archimedes' milk dish to show the cat how to lap up royal milk. The animal, in a fit of savage territoriality, had attacked and clawed the king. "I have been unable to speak," the king explained to the queen, "because the cat got my tongue."

Cliché Number Two

Muriel and Arnold Frump, an upscale couple with a lavish spread in Palm Springs, were bored. Their children were grown. They had refurbished the yacht. What was left? Then Muriel hit on the bright idea: "How about a luxury spa for pets? "Brilliant," said Arnold. "There's money in pets." And with that, the world-famous luxury spa The Paws That Refreshes was born.

No amenity was spared. There was even a fat farm for cats who, after a week-long hundred-calorie-a-day diet, would be returned to their Gucci-clad owners Siamese-slim.

There was just one problem. The Palm Springs heat sometimes incapacitated the pampered pets, so the Frumps installed an air-conditioned pet lounge and romping track atop the Kadillac Kennels, the spa's choicest accommodations located just alongside the Frump house itself.

One day during a particularly intense heat spell, the air-conditioning gave out. The pampered pets, panting, listless, and beside themselves with heat exhaustion, found an opening at the side of the rooftop kennel, looked down at the Frump's tantalizing swimming pool, and dove in. At precisely the same moment, a sudden violent summer rainstorm struck, causing the housekeeper to look out the window and exclaim, "My Lord, it's raining cats and dogs."

Cliché Number Three

Around the turn of the century, many college fraternities used as part of their initiation rites a game called Cat in the

Bag. After pledges had been put through their paces going out to buy elbow grease, sticking their hands into jars full of "brains," and swallowing goldfish, they were given a large paper bag and told they had to coax the campus cat into the bag or suffer twenty swats on the backside with a paddle.

The pledges were to rely solely on their powers of persuasion. No picking up the cat and placing it in the bag. No sneaking up on the cat and pouncing on it. No enticing it into the bag with catnip or tidbits. In other words, no gimmicks. Each pledge was put on the honor system for the feat but told that the group had its ways of knowing if he cheated. The fraternity brothers, of course, hid in the bushes laughing hysterically as the pledges crawled up to the cat, open bag in hands, chanting, "Here, kitty. Here, kitty. Here, pretty itty kitty."

Once a smart recruit who knew about cat psychology thought he could beat the system. Instead of calling the cat, he simply put the open bag on the ground, told the animal, "Now don't you go into that bag," and walked away. Sure enough, the cat crept into the bag and the pledge quickly snatched it up.

The fraternity brothers hidden in the bushes were shocked. Was this cheating? A quick vote determined it was. So one of them crept up behind the pledge, barked like a dog, and the cat tore out into the night. "Aha, the cat's out of the bag," he cried.

The startled pledge realized the group had seen what he did, and from that day on the term "The cat's out of the bag" referred to being found cheating, and later to telling secrets in general.

Cliché Number Four

In the mid 1950s in England, a Yorkshire carpenter claimed he had taught his pet cat, Virtuoso, to play the piano. He would take Virtuoso to the local pub and astound the customers with the pet's rendition of "The Minute Waltz" played on a tiny puss-sized piano.

Only the bartender knew that the cat, of course, couldn't play a note. The piano was just a miniature variation of the player piano principle. Virtuoso had been trained to bang on the keys in exchange for a hefty post-performance portion of fish and chips. Pressure on the keys triggered the player mechanism, and the carpenter was always careful to keep his cat act safely distant from the audience.

One night, after Virtuoso's fame had mounted sufficiently so that the pub was overflowing with curious customers, everyone insisted on buying the talented cat's owner a drink. Before he knew it, the carpenter had overindulged and passed out. Virtuoso, looking for his usual post-performance treat, wandered off to raid a platter of fish and chips in the kitchen.

The crowd quieted down for a while, when suddenly the tinkling of the piano could be heard again, but instead of Virtuoso at the keyboard, everyone was astonished to see two small white mice prancing energetically up and down on the keys.

"Blimey," said one well-fortified customer. "We have for sure a talented supply of animals in Yorkshire. Look at that. When the cat's away, the mice will play."

Cat Quotations

1. Cats and monkeys, monkeys and cats. All human life is there.—Henry James
Except maybe Howard Cossell.

2. Singing cats and whistling girls will come to a bad end.—English proverb
This is especially true since the demise of Ed Sullivan.

3. The cat loves fish but hates to get his feet wet.— Lady MacBeth
Looks like a market in paw-sized kitty boots for some smart venture capitalist.

4. If you don't own your cat, your cat owns you.— Proverb
Then let the cat pay the mortgage.

5. What is born of a cat catches mice.—Proverb
And deposits them on your pillow at 5:30 A.M.

6. If man could be crossed with a cat, it would improve man but deteriorate the cat.—Mark Twain
Maybe, but would anyone want a pinup of Burt Reynolds with a tail?

7. If you leave the kitchen door open, don't blame the cat for stealing the food.—Old Proverb
Why not? You want we should just let 'em off with a slap on the paws?

8. The way to keep a cat is to try to chase it away— E. W. Howe
A principle also understood by those with nerdy boyfriends.

9. The ideal of calm exists in the sitting cat.— Jules Renard
So why isn't kitty the one with his paw on the Button?

10. If human, cats might play solitaire, but they would never sit around with the gang and a few six-packs watching Monday night football.—*Time* magazine, December 7, 1981
Just as well. There'd be a hell of a rush for the litter box at half time.

Great Moments in Cat History

The Good Book is not specific on which day the Lord created mice, but from all we know we can be sure that whenever it was, the first cat showed up about twelve minutes later.

Ever since, kitties have been scratching and nuzzling at the key events of history, delighting almost as many people as they have irritated. Here is a totally arbitrary selection from the ongoing saga of pussies and people.

A long time ago. Noah's ark leaves port. As usual, cat is
unwilling to come when called.

3500 B.C. Cats given god status in ancient Egypt, continue to work wrath in the usual places.

1700. Demonstrating an interest not only in what goes up and down but also what goes in and out, Sir Isaac Newton invents the cat door.

1750. Cats officially imported to American colonies to fight rodents.

1872. First cat show held at the Crystal Palace in London. Well-bred cats leave 98 percent of crystal intact.

1875. Johannes Brahms, no friend of cats, regularly takes a break from composing to practice cat archery from his window.

(c. 1940) Cat litter invented.

1969. Morris saved from untimely demise at animal shelter when talent scout notices the cat's uncanny ability to keep his cool.

1971. D. E Gordon Altman, a cat, is elected to student senate at Southern Illinois University on a platform of expanding rat control and solving the dog problems on campus.

1973. California governor Ronald Reagan signs a state law that can send a person to prison for kicking and injuring a cat.

The Literary Cat

For the cat lover, warehouses of cat literature accurately document cat treks across continents and pussies' mythic bouts with gargantuan doses of catnip. A surplus of writers is available who will not miss an orifice as they lead you through kitty's regular bathing ritual.

But there is also another, less realistic body of cat literature in which art is definitely not imitating life.

Here we expose some discrepancies between some famous literary cats and their real-life counterparts.

In fiction	*In real life*
The Cat in the Hat brings out his magic machine to repair all the damage he has done in the house.	About all you can do really is move a few pillows around.
Rudyard Kipling writes of the cat who says "All places are alike to me."	To your real pussy the top underwear drawer is not quite like any place else.
The Cheshire cat grinned when he saw Alice.	A grin requires at least a couple of chicken breasts, never mind Alice.
Dick Wittington got rich off his cat's mousing.	Today you have to be a vet, a groomer, or a cat mortician to get rich off cats.
The owl and the pussycat marry and then go to sea in a beautiful pea-green boat.	Pussycats aren't much for ceremony. They skip the preliminaries and get right down to business.
Garfield predictably scarfs lasagne.	When it comes to what cats will scarf, all bets are off.
T.S. Eliot's "Practical Cats" was made into a musical.	Your cat is more likely to just make music at an impractical hour.

In fiction	*In real life*
Puss in Boots gave the king exotic gifts in the name of his master.	The only thing a cat is likely to give you or anyone else is fleas.
The idealistic Don Quixote addressed a couple of cats that had leaped on a knight's nose, "Avaunt, ye witchcraft-worn rabble."	Most people now would yell "Scat," with the same results.
In fiction Dick and Jane run to see Puff.	There is no need to run. Puff isn't going anywhere. He'll just be sleeping on the window seat like every afternoon.

The Kitty Hit Parade

"Three Blind Mice"

"Bewitched, Bothered, and Bewhiskered"

"Felines (Nothing More Than Felines)"

"Fleas, Release Me"

"I'm Gonna Wash That Tom Right Out of My Fur"

"Tuna, Tuna" (sung to the tune of the Yale University fight song)

CHAPTER 7
Accessories and A-cat-rements

The Unofficial List of Cat Records

Most cats are pretty unassuming about their accomplishments. A kitty contender for the world mouse-catching title, for instance, is likely to project a Joe Montana "Shucks, it's no big deal" demeanor.

It is just because so many pussies are self-effacing that we feel compelled to celebrate some remarkable individual achievements by members of the cat community.

World's champion water lapper: Natasha, a Russian Blue from Englewood Cliffs, New Jersey, has been known to take 435 little sips of water

to a single swallow. Lately, Natasha has been pursued by literary agents who claim, "There must be a diet book there somewhere."

Most accomplished starer: Empress, the cat who could make a zombie blink first, has gazed unflinchingly at humans for up to two hours, a degree of visual fixation rivaled only by six-year-olds watching Saturday morning cartoons.

World's most flexible cat: Jelly Belly, of Petaluma, California, is the world's most hang-loose champion, having contorted himself into positions formerly accomplished only by the Rubber Man of Sumatra. Jelly Belly is currently working on challenging the old saying, "It will happen the day a cat licks its ear."

Longest unescorted trip: Tom-Tom, now of Vancouver, holds the record for his cross-country sojourn to follow his owners from Florida to Washington. Whether his trip was motivated by love of his owners or the prospect of finding high-quality salmon is a question hotly debated by experts.

Champion shedder: Electra holds the world's one-month shedding championship record at seven bushels, an amount said to be equivalent to the amount of hair dislodged by an average size rock group who decide to get daytime jobs.

Most nurturing cat father: As we go to press, Felix, a Japanese Bobtail from Decatur, Illinois, has been spotted on three consecutive days in the same block as the litter he sired. In the cat world, this degree of fatherly solicitude puts Felix right up there with Dr. Cliff Huxtable.

World's yawning champion: Dinah holds the yawning record with a clocked twenty-nine yawns in one minute, a talent particularly valued by her owners, who enlist their cat's aid in dispersing boring guests.

Longest leap from one precarious perch to another: Colonel, of Salt Lake City, Utah, leapt an amazing forty-two feet from the top of a clock radio in the bedroom to a hanging macramé planter in the kitchen next door. Although now called the Evil Knievel of the cat world, according to Colonel's owner, "He was never much of a daredevil before. I think he just got fed up with listening to Top Forty DJs."

The Whole Cat Cat-a-log

We know cat owners are busy watching their pussies chase flies around the window with their paws or chew on carpet fluff. With all this excitement going on at home, who wants to go out and shop?

That's why the Whole Cat Cat-a-log. The Whole Cat Cat-a-log saves pet owners the trouble of chasing all over town looking for the latest cat collectible or the best birthday gift for puss. All the items in the Whole Cat Cat-a-log *are* the latest and the best. Take our word for it.

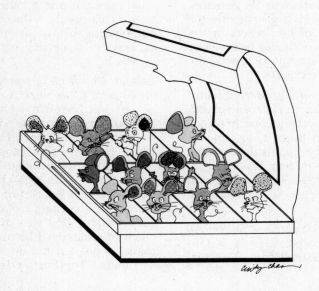

Boxed Mice. No longer do you need to send your pet into dingy basements and dangerous back alleys to get the taste treat he truly craves. Surprise him with his very own set of ranch-grown boxed mice, scrumptious delicacies hand-selected by a team of the country's top gourmet cats. Plain or with insect garnish.

The Mom Cat Hot Water Bottle. Kitty always nuzzling in your armpit to get warm? Cuddling in the microwave? Appropriating the electric heater? Then give your pet the Mom Cat Hot Water Bottle, a dream-come-true gift. Shaped like good old mom, complete with fur-trimmed tummy, the Mom Cat Hot Water bottle will keep your kitty contentedly purring through the chilliest days.

Consolation Prize Ribbons for Cat Show Losers. Pussy pouting because he lost at the cat show? No need. Give your pet his very own consolation prize ribbon. Specially manufactured for pet show losers, these bright blue ribbons feature a large "Number 1 Cat." Puss will be so proud he'll never notice the fine print designating him Number 1 cat at your address. More than one cat? No problem. Ribbons can be imprinted with each puss's name—for example, "Number 1 cat named Taffy at 123 Main Street."

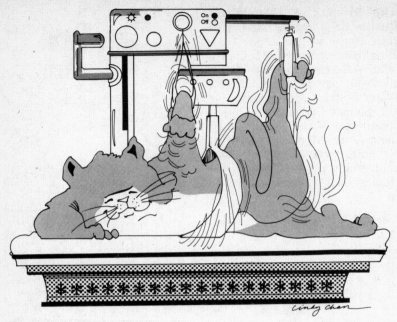

Cat Gym. Ideal for the pussy who is just a nudge pudgy and for the truly fat cat alike. Special design allows cat to recline or even nap while working out. Unique mechanism does all the work. Lever arms raise and lower puss's paws and legs while a wide vibrating band around his middle tones up sagging tummy muscles. Kitty is free to daydream or snooze while shaping up.

Fur Extender. Watch the neighborhood bullies run when you equip your pet with the fabulous Fur Extender. This specially designed fur-enhancing mousse, based on the formula developed for Tina Turner, can double kitty's size in seconds during those all-too-frequent confrontations with macho toms and panting pit bulls. Handy dispenser doubles as collar ornament.

Hologram of Your Living Room. Delight your pet with a room of his own where he can shred the sofa, pee on the rug, and gobble up the goldfish for dinner. A living room hologram will fool even the slyest of cats into thinking he has won the war over territory. Meanwhile, regain the real living room for use with polite company. End forever the irritating ritual of having to throw India prints on the sofa and flick fleas off the curried salmon dip. A gift for the whole family if ever there was one.

Cat Wigs. Now no cat needs to go through life as an ugly short-haired wallflower. New 100 percent cat fur wigs can transform even the homeliest alley cat into a long-haired beauty. Available in styles ranging from Turkish Angora to Maine Coon. Zip-on or Velcro closings.

Adjustable Paw Extender. Ever notice how kitty always wants the unattainable—the fly on the ceiling or the cherry to-

mato behind the stove? Now you can put an end to this perennial pussy frustration. The adjustable paw extender can provide kitty with extra reaching power ranging from two inches to twelve feet. Simple, quiet push-button drive allows kitty's paw to stretch and snatch an unsuspecting mouse or snitch a pickled herring from the house next door.

Today's Special - Liver Mouse Delight

☐ Spicy Chilled Mousy Tail

☐ Mousy Morsels

☐ Blackbirds Banquet

☐ Sparrow Surprise

☐ Minced Mole and Ferret

Fish Eyes Soup ☐

Mixed Grilled - ants, house flies, and fur balls ☐

Fish Heads ☐

Basic Cat Gruel with Grass ☐

Basic Cat Gruel

Scratch and Sniff Menu. Tired of kitty skulking away with contempt from the industrial meat remnants with artificial gravy that he loved last week? Tried everything you know to serve his food just right—not too hot or too cold, not too bland or too smelly, not too dry or too runny? Then try the scratch and sniff menu, a revolutionary way to figure out what kitty wants to eat *today*. Kitty simply scratches menu patches to sample treats as varied as tuna smorgasbord surprise and liver by-products banquet. When kitty scratches and smiles, bingo. That's today's entree. Menu comes with twenty-four-pack box of Happy Cat Cuisine.

Fake Cord for Celluar Phones.

Pussy bored? Those new cordless phones may have increased the mobility of phone-using cat owners, but they greatly inhibit the fun for the cat who likes to play with the cord. Now it is possible to buy kitty a fake cord to attach to your cellular phone so the puss can tangle it just as in the old days. When you get a call, simply detach the phone from the cord, leaving kitty to scramble happily with the tangle.

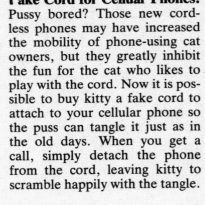

Electric Eye Cat Door.

Give your cat the independence he's always wanted. The revolutionary new electric eye cat door allows your puss to achieve a state of equilibrium he has only dreamed of before. Now he can be inside and outside simultaneously.

Cat Answering Machine. This is just the thing for cat owners who miss their pussies while at work. The cat answering machine allows owners to contact their kittens several times a day to give instructions and purr endearments. Machine may be customized with owner's portrait, which sometimes fools very dumb cats.

Cat Condoms. Help your puss become a responsible member of the cat community while at the same time allowing him to express the animal in himself. Supply him with cat condoms specially treated with a catnip scent guaranteed to drive his mating partners wild. Soon all the female felines in town will insist that their toms use these seductive condoms, thus helping to bring down the homeless kitty population. Attractive ringlike condom case attaches to puss's back paw for ease of application.

Morris's Favorite Films

The Man Who Loved Cat Dancing

A Litter from Three Wives

That Darn Cat

Cat on a Hot Tin Roof

Cat People

Gay Purr-ee

Cat Ballou

Honorable Mention

Bringing Up Baby

Born Free

The Lion in Winter

A Fish Called Wanda

Cat-ch 22

The Big Sleep

Fur Me and My Gal

Alternative Careers for the Discriminating Tabby

Paperweight

Freudian analyst

Chief stamp licker, mailroom

Mattress tester

Night watchman

Vice-president of the United States

Puss's Favorite Books

The Power of Pawsitive Thinking

Caterbury Tails

Grimms Furry Tails

Davy Crock-cat

Cat-cher in the Rye

A Tail of Two Kitties

Quotations of Meow-Tse-Tung

The Torn Birds

No More Waiting For Mr. (Ms.) Goodpuss

If you have read this far in *The Unofficial Cat Owner's Handbook* and still own no kitty with whom to share the remains of your chicken breast cabernet, you have only yourself to blame.

Stop making excuses. It's just not true that all the good cats are either married or gay. In fact, none of them are either. And don't buy the myth that sharing your life with a kitty will distract you from your climb up the corporate ladder. Who else will be willing to monitor the 5 a.m. rehearsal of your flip chart presentation to the stockholders? Your cat will create no professional problems that cannot be solved with a high quality lint remover.

But, of course, you'll need to be careful. Those charming pusses you run into at the bus stop—the ones who are all leg rubs and Valentino eyes—may not be ready for commitment. Unfortunately, there will always be a high percentage of pussies who are only interested in catting around.

So what is the potential cat owner, hungry for a serious relationship, to do? As it turns out, cat attendance at church socials, never impressive, has been particularly off in these secular times. And as the unromantic types who manage supermarkets seldom allow a pussy through the door, you are not likely to bump into your dream pussy hanging around the Johnny Cat display.

No, if there are going to be any feline fireworks in your life, you are going to have to set them off. And as the makers of Purina, Kal Kan, and Nine Lives might tell you, where cats are concerned, it pays to advertise. Here is a model personal ad to get you started.

Kiss Me Kat

Sensuous kitty person, tired of meowless mornings, wants to share barepaw walks on the beach with that special kitty. If you are a non-smoking cat, not afraid of commitment, willing to trade the swinging lifestyle for cuddles in front of the VCR, naps in a warm lap, and exclusive use of a top-of-the-line climbing tower, come scratch on my door. Let's have a claws encounter of the best kind. No catnip junkies, please. Write Lady Caterly's Lover, PO Box 123456789.

RIB-TICKLING HANDBOOKS

☐ **THE UNOFFICIAL MOTHER'S HANDBOOK** by Norma and Art Peterson. The essential guide for the only person who ever applauded when you went to the bathroom; the adjudicator of who hit whom first; the person known to begin sentences with "You'll be sorry when . . ." Here is an affectionately funny survey of motherhood from "day 1" through "leaving the nest" and "are you back again?"   (262461—$6.95)

☐ **THE OFFICIAL M.D. HANDBOOK** by Anne Eva Ricks, M.D. Are you M.D. material? Find out with this hilarious handbook of tricks and secrets of the medical trade. Dr. Ricks offers an irreverent and humorous look at the life of a doctor, from med school to malpractice insurance.   (254388—$4.95)

☐ **THE UNOFFICIAL NURSE'S HANDBOOK** by Nina Schroeder, R.N., with Richard Mintzer. Find out what makes a nurse tick! Nina Schroeder will have you in stitches as she introduces you to the best and worst moments in a nursing career. From favorite nurse entertainment to famous phrases they teach in nursing school, the contents of this book are guaranteed to split your sides.   (258995—$6.95)